PSYCHO POETICA

EDITED BY
SIMON BARRACLOUGH

For Inua,
Nice to meet you!
Simon
York 2012

SIDEKICK BOOKS
www.drfulminare.com

Published in 2012 by
SIDEKICK BOOKS
Flat 38, 23 Mile End Road
London E1 4TN

Printed by EX WHY ZED

Typeset in Myriad Pro, with Movie Poster and Hitchcock

Copyright of text remains with authors

Simon Barraclough has asserted his right to be identified as editor of this work under Section 77 of the Copyright, Designs and Patents Act 1988.

All rights reserved.

No part of this book may be reproduced, stored in a retrieval system of transmitted in any form without the written permission of Sidekick Books

ISBN: 978-0-9564164-8-3

~

ACKNOWLEDGEMENTS
Twelve of these poems were originally published in *The Manhattan Review* Vol. 14, No. 2 Fall/Winter 2010-11. Several of these poems have been published in the poets' independent collections.

CONTENTS

Introduction / 4

THE MAIN FEATURE
MATTHEW WELTON - Untitled / 10
DZIFA BENSON - The $40,000 Pill / 12
SIMON BARRACLOUGH - Being a Woman You Will / 15
HEATHER PHILLIPSON - 1960s Monochrome Hollywood Paraphernalia ($47, collection only) / 17
RICHARD PRICE - Only My Share / 19
JANE DRAYCOTT - Untitled / 22
EMILY BERRY - The Birds on the Wall Point Two Ways / 24
CHRIS MCCABE - Untitled / 26
JOE DUNTHORNE - Dear Arbogast / 29
LUKE HEELEY - Cabin Number One / 32
ISOBEL DIXON - Trappings / 34
ANNIE FREUD - The Yes and the No and the Terrible Thank You / 37

ALTERNATIVE TAKES
RODDY LUMSDEN - What the Shrimp Calls Its Tail, I Call Its Handle / 40
LIANE STRAUSS - Everything is Black and White / 41
JOHN STAMMERS - Mop and Pail / 43
EMILY BERRY - The House by the Railroad / 44
ISOBEL DIXON - California Gothic / 45
CATHERINE SMITH - She Sits Like a Bird / 46

Cast in order of appearance / 48

INTRODUCTION

W<small>HEN</small> I was nine years old, as my parents left for a Saturday night out, my mother warned me: "Don't watch that evil film on television at 9 o'clock." So of course my babysitting sister and I counted down the minutes to 9 o'clock and began to watch the film we didn't even know at the time was *Psycho*. Out of a mixture of obedience and fear, we flicked back and forth between channels, growing increasingly scared and intrigued.

I remember rain on a windscreen, stuffed crows, a mop in a bathtub, a car's number plate in the mud, a blackened Gothic pile with a blonde woman slowly approaching it in close-up. None of it made sense but we were too jumpy to stay with it. Years later, when I finally saw the whole thing in one go, that strange sense of dislocation and fragmentation remained: it's ingrained in the visuals, the narrative and the characters. It's what the film is about.

Saul Bass's opening credits and Bernard Herrmann's score set the tone. Horizontal and vertical bars slash the screen on their menacing, driven mission. The words themselves split, jag and disintegrate as they try to signify. This jagged aesthetic continues through the film as space, plots, identities and destinies are flung together and torn apart. Even time is shattered: 45 seconds never passed more slowly yet more energetically than they do in cinema's most memorable scene.

My fascination with Hitchcock endured: I wrote several poems inspired by his films, his style, and even the tag lines of the films' posters. So it seemed natural to mark the 50th anniversary of *Psycho* with some kind of poetic celebration. I approached Mark Reid of the British Film Institute for support. Mark is a keen poetry fan and I had already worked alongside other poets on his BFI Mediatheque project *O Dreamland*. He was interested in principle, but first I needed to find a way in: the right approach to *Psycho Poetica*.

I considered commissioning general poems about *Psycho* and perhaps inviting speakers to a poetic conference, but then I remembered that first encounter and realised that I needed to fragment the film again. I could 'slash' it into segments and allot one each to twelve poets ("Twelve cabins, twelve vacancies", to quote Norman Bates). In my grander visions, I imagined a one-minute poem for each minute of the film, giving us around 109 poets and 109 poems in 109 minutes. Maybe one day.

The poets I invited to the project were a mixture of people I'd worked with before; poets I wanted to work with; poets who had shown interest in collaborations and filmic projects in the past; poets I'd known for years, and poets I'd never met. Over the course of five performances to date, the 'cast' has changed because the original 12 weren't always available, so in the end 16 poets were involved. Every time I invited a new poet, I requested a new poem, which is why this anthology contains 18 poems (Emily Berry eventually wrote poems for two segments and Isobel Dixon wrote an additional 'spoiler-free' poem for her segment; more on that later).

Watching and pausing on DVD, I divided the film into roughly nine-minute segments. I put these timings into one hat and the names of 12 poets into another hat (real hats by the way). As I was allotting these scenes, I realised that there isn't a single dull moment in the film.

The poets' task was to write a poem in close response to their segments, without reference to anything they knew of happening before or after it. I discouraged consultations between the poets. I wanted them to 'write to the moment' of the scene, following any poetic impulse it generated. The aim was to perform the 12 poems together as a sequence, without titles or introductions, to create a parallel poetic version, or 'a faithful distortion', of *Psycho*.

We selected still images to contextualise each poem and I commissioned a new piece of music from Oli Barrett of Bleeding Heart Narrative to divide the reading between the sixth and seventh poems. His piece 'Cop Shy' is a cunning homage to the Hermann original, played by an unusual string quartet comprised of one violin and three cellos (Clarissa Carlyon, Simon Trevethick and Phil Noyce played along with Oli at the first four performances).

The BFI was happy with this approach and, thanks to contacts at LOVEFiLM and The Whitechapel Gallery, I managed to raise further funding. More support came later from the Latitude Festival, Tilt and, in 2012, StAnza InternationalPoetry Festival.

Psycho Poetica premiered at the British Film Institute in London on 10 April 2010 to a packed house. Another performance with a slightly different line-up followed at The Whitechapel Gallery on 13 May.

Reactions to this second performance made me think that perhaps the show could be more tightly integrated. The best way to do this seemed to be to score it all, so Oli Barrett very generously (and very quickly) composed individual music for each poem.

The whole piece would now be read to original, sensitively-scored music that worked with the rhythm and tone of each poem. This was the version we performed at the Latitude Festival in July 2010. Because the music was written specially for the 12 poems we read at Latitude, it has become the 'fixed' sequence of *Psycho Poetica*. This is the version you can read in 'The Main Feature' section. There is no 'best' version and it's important to read the alternative poems for a slightly different journey.

The 'Latitude' version was performed again at The Royal Festival Hall as part of Tilt's 'Something I Said' spoken word festival and in March 2012 Isobel Dixon, Joe Dunthorne and I performed a 'portable' version of the show using pre-recorded music at the StAnza Festival in St Andrews. My initial aim was to perform the piece at least twice, so I'm delighted that we were able to expand, refine and perform the show at different venues over the last two years.

So here are a few tasting notes for the twelve poems in 'The Main Feature'. Any thematic or stylistic links between adjacent poems were entirely coincidental.

Matthew Welton's untitled poem covers the main titles and reproduces a sense of Saul Bass's design: splinters, repetitions, parallels, borders, energy. There's even a nod to Hitchcock's cameo in the "Inordinately familiar. Passingly profile." Dzifa Benson picks up the baton of Welton's Marion and takes her on a moral fugue "From Arizona to California on a wing and not enough/prayer." The poem is aptly and 'accidentally' stuffed with bird references.

My Marion is "a conjoined only twin/connected at the deed" who meets Heather Phillipson's Norman Bates in '1960s Monochrome Hollywood Paraphernalia ($47, collection only)'. The birds return, along with the chaotic paraphernalia of this fractured antihero whose revealed psyche begins to feel like some kind of forlorn yard sale: "1 little frequented plot / of mud. 1 woman's voice (disembodied). / Sturdy rain (evidently trying to prove / something). My trusty umbrella."

Richard Price intensifies the growing unease with his spiky poem (and spiky performance of) 'Only My Share' with its subtle deformations of original dialogue: "I bet you've never had a hobby in your life." and "Do you know what I think? / If you love someone you hate them."

How do you write about the shower scene; the scene that perhaps everybody wanted but feared getting? Jane Draycott's take is cool and original; folkloric and touching: "High above the tree-line in a cave / of ice there lies a field of untouched snow, / and rushing headwaters, the *fons et origo*." See the 'Alternative Takes' section for Liane Strauss's very different treatment of this pivotal segment.

Emily Berry returns us to the fragmentary style we opened with, and attention shifts back to Norman. He usurps the sequence, as he usurps the film, with a disturbing lyric of guilt and helplessness: "Lovely Up to Your Neck, Up to Your Eyes." Chris McCabe turns the menace up to full volume with his steely monologue and its fixation on the blurred identity of Norman Bates. A pitch black humour shimmers, watched over by "The crow. The owl. The lamp. The safe." In performance, I've seen people flinch at this section.

Joe Dunthorne floats up the staircase with Arbogast, taunting the memorably doomed investigator with a sardonic yet sympathetic wit: "Don't look so surprised, Arbogast, / I've known you were dead for decades, / nice of you to catch up." Luke Heeley slows the pace with characteristic philosophical delicacy: the calm before the coming storm. "Time is stashed in the bedside drawer / where it's slowed to sap, to glue, to cement."

By the time we get to Isobel Dixon's poem 'Trappings', we're with Lila, Marion's sister; similar, but no twin. Like Lila, the poem opens doors into the Bates House, approximately one door per stanza. All these rooms take her and us deeper into the mystery and closer to the film's great reveal: "The mystery of stairs, and doors, / all five that Lila opens, / sense on sense, sharpened / by strings."

The End is upon us and Annie Freud delivers a plaintive, personal closer with a chuckle of morbid wit and an adagio of sadness: "We are almost at the end. / I can go back to my own swamp / and its wise-cracking inhabitants, / their stitches coming loose."

But this is not the end. Continue to 'Alternative Takes' for six extra poems, which were all performed at least once as part of the show. In the week of the premiere, a few of us were lucky enough to introduce the film *Psycho* to audiences at the BFI and, realising that some people may not know who's lurking in the cellar, Isobel wrote a new poem, 'California Gothic', which doesn't give anything away. As Hitchcock said: "Don't give away the ending, it's the only one we've got."

The final words of 'The Main Feature' are "Thank you" and it remains for me to thank all the poets and musicians who worked on the project and all those who made its performance possible: The BFI, LOVEFiLM, The Whitechapel Gallery, Latitude Festival, Tilt and StAnza. Finally, thanks to Jon Stone and Kirsten Irving of Sidekick Books.

SIMON BARRACLOUGH, AUGUST 2012

8

0:00:00 > 0:09:12

MATTHEW WELTON
UNTITLED

Slowly and gray and a sidewalk alongside.
Items in a landscape; items in hotels.
Subtitles is people gathering hurriedly when.

And laze around a lunch hour. Sure talk and last time.
Items on a table; items on a chair.
Movies is possible. And letters and trips is possible.

Sometimes a while, and a big steak sometimes.
Items in place. Items on a bed.
Under any circumstances, interested is having to be.

                                      Portly on a sidewalk. Standing inordinately.
                                          Inordinately familiar. Passingly profile.
                                              Profile sidewalk. Passingly passingly.

                              A gentleman and passingly. Passingly inordinately.
                                    A not inordinately passingly portly.
                                      A gentleman familiar. And not a what.

Take a look at Marion. Marion over the
Weekend. Monday morning Marion. You forget them as
Soon as. Watching him turn Marion. Lunching with

The man who. Get him to give us
A Marion instead. When he found out I'd
Taken the Marion. Forty thousand Marion. This size

Is most irregular. That's not Marion. I get
To keep Marion. Got a headache. You got
Some aspirin. You girls oughtta get. It's my

Private Marion. Relaxes her Marion. A thing like that – speaking
Of feeling. My mother called Marion. Suppose we put it
In. Sometimes I can keep my Marion shut.

0:09:13 > 0:18:00

DZIFA BENSON
THE $40,000 PILL

I runne to death, and death meets me as fast, and all my pleasures are like yesterday; I dare not move my dim eyes any way.
JOHN DONNE, HOLY SONNET 1

Stifling in your apartment Marion
you can't hold your own gaze in the mirror.
Sun shines but it's not for you, even your own shadow
trips before you.

Thirty plus with a yen for hardware store dealers,
too old to grab for lunchtime gropes on the side.
Too sick to pander to loudmouth highrollers
with nothing to declare but the flash of cold, hard cash.

Little league blonde, girl Friday ten years in the making
ordinary woman, extraordinary temptation. Take one
last gasp to fit the skin of the American Dream before
it jump cuts to black.

Get the hell out of dodge, white bird, take flight
go to seed to get hitched in black torpedo bra. Before
you leave Marion, be sure to turn Mama's eyes
to the wall.

Lowery, askance at the crosswalk while the die
casts your face glazed, the twist in your gut knits
the flat planes of your perky mug, and that headache
still woodpeckers away.

Two days on the lam, in a black '56 Ford Mainline, desert
highway yawns cacti and white lines. Check your status
in rear-view, eyes fixed, clench the steering wheel
will Sam be pleased to see you?

All that driving, inner voices clamouring, that bitten
lip and gnawed finger. Violas breathe hard, stringing
and plucking dread over your mind and that wad
of greenbacks stashed in your black handbag.

From Arizona to California on a wing and not enough
prayer. We can't see you or your white picket fence
in John Law's aviators. Look! His car's a raven black hulk
in your rear-view mirror.

Hurtling from headaches to headlights, U-turns
and headlines, a magpie in car reg. ANL-709.
You can't buy off unhappiness with pills, you said.
Marion, you should have spent the weekend in bed.

0:18:01 > 0:27:02

SIMON BARRACLOUGH
BEING A WOMAN YOU WILL

do anything you've a mind to.
First customer of the day's not *the* but *in* the most trouble.
The over-the-state-line headlines blank, thankfully,
you. You hinge upon the mirror at the elbow
in the Ladies' Room. For a moment
you've stolen twice as much, bitten off far more.
You're a conjoined only twin

connected at the deed.
In God We Trust, with automatic fingers, seven times for luck.
See if something strikes your eyes.
The pennants show their teeth in California Charlie's sky.
You try and fail to lose your baggage;
the things you've done could give you whiplash;
you flee from salesman, cop, mechanic.

This road ahead's the only thing that's real;
your past life's back-projected now.
Across your knuckles darkness silts
as asphalt miles fall underneath the wheels.
The voices in your head begin;
there's one demands your fine soft flesh.
The further away, the louder they get.

The wiper blades will never shift this weight
of water. Headlights splat against the shield
like Rorschach tests in negative
and while you try to work them out
the highway goes and pulls its rug from under you.
Tiredness kills. It's time to find a place to stay.
Dirty night. They'll never hear you in this rain.
Try the horn. Seven times for luck.
Do anything you've a mind to.

0:27:03 > 0:35:58

HEATHER PHILLIPSON
1960S MONOCHROME HOLLYWOOD PARAPHERNALIA ($47, COLLECTION ONLY)

• **1 sizeable hoard** of defunct birds (some deader than others). Includes an owl (unusually rigid) and anything else you would want to see in flight in spring (mounted, in a parlour). All come with tiny bones walloped into a museum of artistic poses (if you lean in you can hear innards or the sky curdle steeply). In addition, a period of hurley-burley just beginning. Anticipation that just kind of hovers overhead like an arched eyebrow or a buzzard before supper. A kind of rigorous love. Also: shadows (what they are and what goes on in them). Darkness, generally. (A lot of clouds bumping around the periphery.) Undertones. Overtones. Violin strings (lightly scratched) in upper registers. Blanched hair of a certain period. Tiny gloss eyes pinned in the middle distance. Miscellaneous beaks and a man's mouth, all in nipping distance. 1 devilishly wet December to accompany a tight-fitting office, unlikely to change (unless papers get shuffled). Plus: Pale-faced loon from motel foyer (comes with upturned collar, undernourished, bearing sandwiches). Could I ... uh ... do you ... uh ... here's the ... uh ... (classic examples of awkward speech patterns). 1 little-frequented plot of mud. 1 woman's voice (disembodied). Sturdy rain (evidently trying to prove something). My trusty umbrella.

0:35:59 > 0:45:00

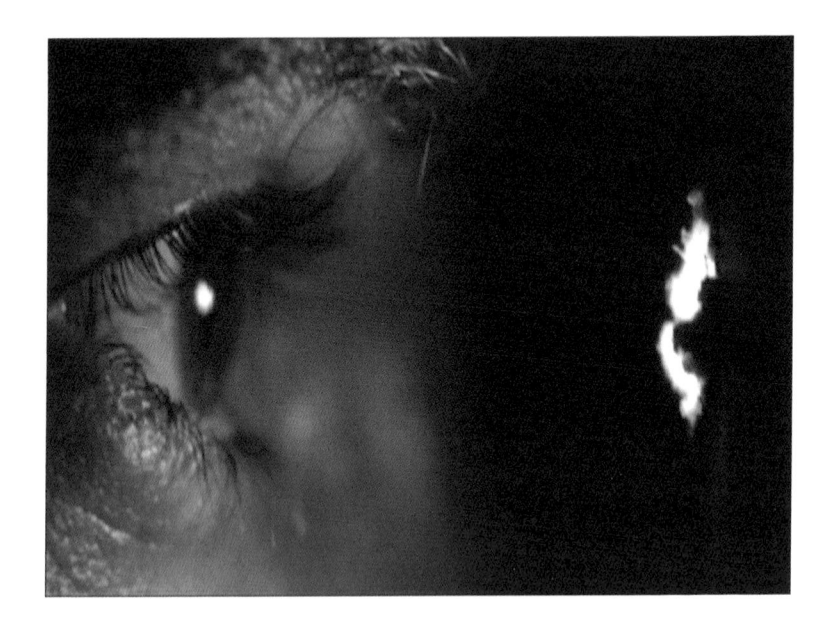

RICHARD PRICE
ONLY MY SHARE

Do you know what I think?
A boy's best friend is I do.
A boy's best friend is a private island.
A boy's best friend is curse her.

I bet you've never had an empty moment in your life.
Only my scratch,
only my claw.
Nothing to talk about, only my share.

Do you know what I think?
We're all in our Security Bank of Phoenix.
We're all a little mad sometimes?
Miss Crane, Marie Samuels.

I bet you've never had a hobby in your life.
Only my scratch,
only my claw.
Nothing to talk about, only my share.

Thoughts and frames, traps and blames.
People click their thick tongues and call it caring.
You wouldn't believe the lives they lead,
the selfishness they call daring.
They can shower, hour on hour, scrub unsparing –
but a flirt is always dirt, however clean she seems, whatever
    layer she's wearing,
and no layer.

Do you know what I think?
If you love someone you hate them.
There are cruel eyes in the institution, laughing – and tears.
A boy's best friend is I do, but I say I don't.

I bet you've never cared for anyone in your life.
Only my scratch,
only my claw.
Nothing to talk about, only my share.
Nothing, nothing to talk about,
only my share.

Alternative take: page 40

0:45:01 > 0:54:06

JANE DRAYCOTT
UNTITLED

High above the tree-line in a cave
of ice there lies a field of untouched snow,
and rushing headwaters, the *fons et origo*

that is the farthest any girl should go
alone. No words are spoken here
or can explain what always happens next.

Free-flying in your naked self – and that's
pure pleasure – in the water's rills and tendrils,
you are in paradise, like heaven on earth

then vision or nightmare, it's as close as that,
the spirit of the woods appears to cut you down.
Woodcutter, granny or wolf, it isn't clear –

enough to know that things have gone too far
and all too soon you're with the angels
which is where the money is as well.

Right now the casement's open to the night
and any creature with a spark of life
could fly right out and still get back to Phoenix

but this woodland has you in its lure,
the eglantine and roses on the walls,
the swallow and the nightjar all declare

this garden is a place to rest, get back
to nature, back to who you really are
beneath those dusty travelling clothes.

And so you end up in the place perpetual
where water is the single syllable that rises
from the ashes, all that lasts after the blast

which comes from nowhere like an August breeze,
comes from beyond the window, from a land
of boiling cloud and altogether bigger trees.

Alternative take: page 41

0:54:07 > 1:03:00

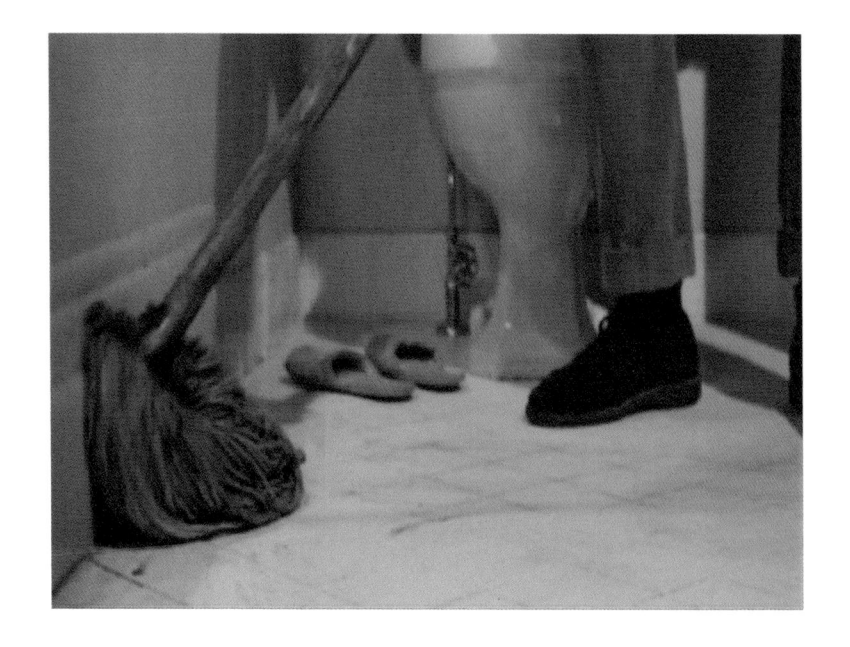

EMILY BERRY
THE BIRDS ON THE WALL POINT TWO WAYS

This is what happens when innocence tilts   the curtains hang
with a new menace   and somebody's had it   Dearest Slowly Sinking
I am less guilty than he is, believe me   I swear by these wallpaper prints

I had these thoughts: a car is always   more or less   like a woman
and your face was your car's cartoon face   with big black eyes   a button nose
and oblong mouth like a letterbox   all the way to the lake

you spelled out his name   lest we forget who drove you to the edge   where
shadows flung themselves across you –   leaf shapes   and giant eyelashes
and finally   the figure of a man caressingly   but they couldn't save you

neither could I   I was too busy writing this letter   I knew less than the rain
and furniture   Lovely Up to Your Neck, Up to Your Eyes   I did not   bend
away from the mirror and into the light   I did not   carry your shoes   push you

into a black   slick place where water oiled itself   and even trees
 were heartless   I did not smile when my plan worked   right to the end
you stared out   blackly   it was hard to tell   who you blamed

Alternative take: page 43

1:03:01 > 1:12:21

25

CHRIS MCCABE
UNTITLED

The crow. The owl. The lamp. The safe.

Arbogast enters the parlour.

The crow.

The owl.

The safe.

You make a mental picturisation of something & then...

It's Bates' neck that is the object in itself, a parcel of digestive tract,
the pump & flue of how each swallow connects with breath
and gives away what we think, the neck just a hook to hang
truth's fish-hooks on, balm-shaved, each nostril shorn of dust or follicle,
reading his own register for what it shows of himself *to* himself,
eyes wet in the hang-dog irony of knowing the worse he acts
the closer he gets ... the neck flickers its trip-switch of conscious
salivation, arches across the register Wrigleys-cool, swallows
back the dust in specks of white – traceless as the word *cash* – relaxes
at the fluke-joke *She's still not here is she?* That's the part he's sure
about, that lubricates the lies because the language fits, his neck
a windpipe for vowels, a suction-pump for candies.

There are benefits to a place like this : a motelier who wants to know
why you've come this way, keeps clean sheets, lets you use the phone
at no extra cost, counts the drops you shake off as rain, dexterous
with attention to every detail, a motelier so in control & clean that *you*
feel strange – a story required to say where you've been –
and it drops its cache in sense just why the sign BATES MOTEL [NO]
VACANCY has cancelled its plural because there's only one of you
to check-in, one night like this, one breakfast to go, one cabin, one bed.

One last chance to still be back in an hour, maybe less.

In the parlour the crow is whispering to the owl
whispering the one thing visitors should never know,
that Bates has a vulva inside him, the same one
he was born from, a vulva inside him made of the same
cells he pisses with, a vulva of dry woodwind that sends
him to sleep each night on a rockaby of calm beginnings,
a vulva inside him that is learning to talk, talk freely
through the sacristy of a long open skirt, a vulva
that can't be fooled – especially not by a woman –
a vulva, then, that wants a man? Could Arbogast
be the one with his strong white teeth, Latino grace,
and if Arboghast knew that Bates has a vulva inside him
would he want to know, if only to help with the case?

The lamp's too bright.

 The safe tight shut.

The crow & the owl show Arbogast the silence.

1:12:22 > 1:21:07

JOE DUNTHORNE
DEAR ARBOGAST

If you could see what I can see
or hear the butchered violins,
you'd stop still on the porch,
sniff the air, undoff that fedora,
clack back down the garden steps,
such exactness in your hips
(am I wrong to think you dance?)
take your wide car, drive slowly
on the highway, and phone it in:
"Everything's normal at the Bates Motel."

But you're just too curious.
What burning calculations
made you reach the nineteenth stair?
I'm pinned to the ceiling with worry;
a blade of widening light
slides across the Persian rug.

Don't look so surprised, Arbogast,
I've known you were dead for decades,
nice of you to catch up,
just leave the way you came in, but flailing,
levitating, dolly-tracked, that lick
of new romantic gore as you fall
to the hallway pursued by your killer
in periwinkle blue. You wail like a sick man,
like a bird in a ring-pull, I'm aghast
at your sacrifice, oh please Arbogast,

Arbogast,
          Arbogast, they're calling
your name at the Bates Motel lake.
What words of advice, detective,
as search party follows search party,
chained together by torchlight?

*If you keep knocking and knocking
then soon enough someone will answer.
A close-up is waiting for those who get close.*

They will not listen, Arbogast.
they won't rest until the sheriff's awake.

1:21:08 > 1:30:29

LUKE HEELEY
CABIN NUMBER ONE

Two visitors just out to take the air,
the sullen air of the airtight room
where ashtray and mirror have staged their coup,
her face an effervescent pill, dissolving.
Subtraction is the cleaner's mode:
to swab so only dust's refrenzied.

> *You'll never be able to hold him still*
> *if he doesn't want to be held.*

Time is stashed in the bedside drawer
where it's slowed to sap, to glue, to cement.
Those long, long evenings filed in timber's rings
when the collector oscillated on the hill:
which piece of fruit, which starched white shirt …
Whatever he resolved is locked in the wood.

> *You'll never be able to hold him still*
> *if he doesn't want to be held.*

A hand has straightened the birds on the wall.
One looks one way, one the other.
Bought at a fire sale and frozen in a glade,
they cast their calls into silence's flame.
The artist stuffed them into two dimensions
then turned their eyes from the world.

> *You'll never be able to hold him still*
> *if he doesn't want to be held.*

1:30:30 > 1:37:16

ISOBEL DIXON
TRAPPINGS

Lila keeps her coat on.
Canny, plucky Lila knows
this motel is no place
she wants to stay:
so close to Fairvale
and a world away,
twelve cabins and twelve
vacancies for unwise girls.

Sam looms in suit and tie.
Norman, in rolled up
shirt-sleeves, brilliant white,
tries to play it cool –
but hands stay jammed
in pockets, then his finger
taps the counter-top.
At his jaw, a muscle leaps.

"Mrs Bates?" A sick old
lady's wardrobe shows
a row of modest sleeves.
So much to cover up.
The motel's slats; that mop
propped up among the crates;
a house of jail-stripe wallpaper,
swags, banisters and pleats.

The mystery of stairs, and doors,
all five that Lila opens,
sense on sense, sharpened
by strings. The dressing table's
moulded hands, the mother's imprint,
and a room of small boy's things:
toys, patchwork quilt, an enigmatic
book. No time to turn the page –

"Where is that girl – ?" – she needs
a hiding place: the cellar, bare,
a naked bulb, no tasselled shade
to soften what she looks upon.
The woven shawl, the grey hair
gathered in a careful bun.
And then the turn – the upflung arm,
a lone bulb pendulum,

raking a shrivelled face. No balm
and no disguise for death. Blonde
beauty starts back in the tilting
light and shade; black-and-white
music's whetted sharps spill
from her open mouth, come
ricocheting off the mummy's
scene-consuming empty-socket grin.

Alternative takes: page 44 and 45

1:37:17 > The End

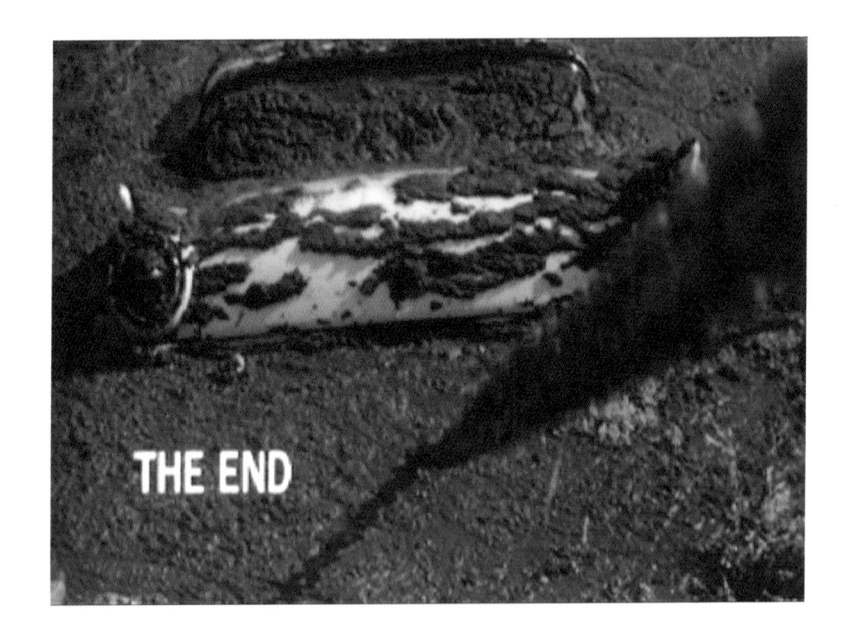

ANNIE FREUD
THE YES AND THE NO AND THE TERRIBLE THANK YOU

I don't know what to say about you.
There is nothing to say about you,
except that you are in my mind,
hideous complexity.

It is only a film that I have watched
too many times, and I have often driven
long distances, worrying about money
and the people I have wronged.

Many films have swamps
with dead bodies hidden in them
and I feel implicated when the car
is winched to the surface.

Then everything will be proven,
the wounds and the weapon,
the approximate times of death,
the missing girls, poor Arbogast.

We are almost at the end.
I can go back to my own swamp
and its wise-cracking inhabitants,
their stitches coming loose.

The psychiatrist's theory is watertight.
She was a clinging, demanding woman.
He was always bad. The *Yes* and the *No*
and Marion, for whom no one cried
and the terrible *Thank you*.

Alternative take: page 46

ALTERNATIVE TAKES

RODDY LUMSDEN
WHAT THE SHRIMP CALLS ITS TAIL, I CALL ITS HANDLE

Will the truth take your weight? Take your weight when you wonder? And when you wear something fragile and spoilable, drop on some silk or push into lace, who is *en garde*? Not the garment, for that's a bimbo thing, unschooled. Not the designer, her feet up in some loft in Milan, surrendered to an empty moment. It's you, then, at fault when it all comes apart. Not the poison we should pay blame to, or the poisoner, who tends to have a decent reason: the poisoned ones are at fault, wretching in a chilly bed of effort, under the cruel eyes of the ward lights, sorry for themselves. And not the trap, laid in long grass so nimbly for noble conclusion; not the self or the stalker who laid it, but you, strolling incumbent, with your halo of fate and your foot just one pace away from the jaws of the truth.

Alternative for 0:35:59 > 0:45:00   (page 18)

LIANE STRAUSS
EVERYTHING IS BLACK AND WHITE

It starts with a house, the ridiculous
gothic house of the fear. Inside he scales
the grand, precipitous, difficult, dark-wood
staircase, the sycophant heights, but only
his eyes. The apple he toys with (will not
dare bite) is the credulous letter, a
score he'll compose in his head but never
settle or write. The trail, like the money,
the proof he needs to tear up (to destroy)
he displays on the wall like delicate
Audubons, hunted and flushed, stuffed, paintbrush
and gun poised to suck the art out of life.

No words are needed. Beauty speaks. Beauty
is here, disrobes, pale as an oyster, poised
like Venus blown clear of the sea by chance
in his dreams, slips out of her slippers, slips
into – behind – the lens out of focus,
the blur of the curtain, the costume, the flesh
the actress wears alone in her shell, feels
fingers of water unlock, unloosen
those lovely curls. There's just one thing he needs
to express. Sh-took. Sh-took. Sh-took. Shh.
The unstiflable tongue in the body
of mouths. "What have you done? What have you –?" Sss-tuck,
says the silencing tongue, the tongue that numbs.
Screech, screech, screech, screech, screams the screech owl's screech.

The tiles are the grave of snow-smothered mud.
Like the wind in his sails from its rigging
torn, the curtain caves in and the whirlpool
drains like passion from flesh, his life, her eye,
from the those were red apples that were her –

Thank God that's over, without the regret.

The house weeps through the shower head. The news
is OKAY. The wallpaper peel doesn't
peal. From the wall a bird flies to the floor.
Still Room Number One. The blushing letters
that buzz and burn and quiver and hum fall
dark and quiet, cold and calm. The long pole
in the mirror is nothing, the handle
of a mop. Just a mess to clean up. Turn
off the watering can that weeps like a
rose. The curtain – pop pop pop – which was
waiting to metamorphose, has become
a body-bag. The red apple returns
as a cold blind eye. These hands. These hands. They're
stubborn as ink in the sink, or a voice
in your – Locks and tresses! Where is that mop?
Mop up, mop up. Roll her up. Roll her up.

For what is beauty that even in death
he cannot hide from what he hides behind
the curtain he wraps her in? The colour
of blood is starker and cleaner in black
and white, the colour of tears, of blood, art.
The naked terror, the pattern of lies,
lies soft and white as white skin on white tiles –
But nothing is white. And nothing is black
if nothing is white, or dead, or alive.
In the winding curtain in which she lies,
she lies, he tells himself, another lie
he tells himself to keep himself from what
he always knew he'd do and done: for, close
the door now, close, he knows he was never
afraid of beauty or ashamed of death.

Alternative for 0:45:01 > 0:54:06 (page 21)

JOHN STAMMERS
MOP AND PAIL

Her lovely shoes in his winsome hand point down, twice.
Mother wouldn't like them, those saucy toes.
Norman has cleaned up with his mop and pail
and Marion's packed up in the trunk of her own car,
the coolest of coffins with tailfins and everything.
And forty-thousand dollars in a rolled-up newspaper.

The car starts to suck into the black amnesia of the swamp,
but it comes to rest, like an inkling at the back of the mind
or a thought about a thing which is not a thing
but a series of blurred images of something else.
The car begins to lose the light, the sweet light, then forgets it entirely.
And the forty-thousand bucks goes down in the car.

In Loomis' store, a lady wants a bug-killer,
insect or man, she opines, death should be painless.
A blond replica of Marion steps in
with her hair all glam like she's at some cocktail party.
Sam looms as only a Sam Loomis can.
I'm Marion's sister; I want to talk about Marion.

Yes, let's talk about Marion, shall we?
It's Arbogast who's come through the door.
He's a private eye with an eye for personal detail.
Who are you friend? demands Sam.
I'm Arbogast, *friend*, so take it easy, *friend*:
someone always see a girl with forty-thousand dollars.

Norman's at home with his stuffed birdlife.
Arbogast shows up and asks him lots of stuff.
One by one you drop the formalities, Norman says,
I hate the smell of dampness, a kind of creepy smell.
Look at this photo, please, Arbogast says to him.
Imagine that: a mop and pail!

Alternative for 0:54:07 > 1:03:00 (page 23)

EMILY BERRY
THE HOUSE BY THE RAILROAD

'This place? This place happens to be my only world.'
— Norman Bates

The house was an old ship moving under me.
It sighed and sighed. Dear House, I said,
whoever lives here has neglected your hopes.
The house looked down with its big round eye
and I stared back, my face was pale as fire.
I was a lantern, rising. I was the one right thing.
This is her room, the house sighed. It was lonely.
In a museum of mirrors and pedestals I walked
and felt the decadent shape of an absent woman.
She was so accounted for, and perfumed. Her
heavy womanliness was like a thump on the
back of the neck. The house was full of wants
and no one had come. I'd opened my arms and it
leaned to me like a ghost that was tired of haunting.
The house rocked itself and mourned. I laid my
hand on the door. But it was too wicked. It hung
my reflection on the wall. The house wanted me
stripped, painted gold and put on a pedestal. It
wanted my delicate hands. I climbed the stairs
with my light. I rose the way a wave does, all gathered
and graceful. A dirty symphony played in the attic.
The house was full of tricks. House, where is she?
I demanded, but the house had gone quiet. I ran
downstairs. I began to know how it feels when
something terrible happens. My kindness had made
the house shiver. I began to fall. The only world
was wrong. I was the highest wave now, I had taken
everything into me and risen up and up. I went through
the rooms in the dark. I thought I had found her.
The moon lit her neat grey hair and I broke. Mother?

Alternative for 1:30:30 > 1:37:16 (page 33)

ISOBEL DIXON
CALIFORNIA GOTHIC

This place happens to be my only world.
  He keeps his shirtsleeves carefully rolled.
Where is that girl you came here with – ?
  He isn't fooled by motel check-in
coupledom, the fabricated register.
  My mother and I were more than happy here.

My mother and I were more than happy here.
  I grew up in that house up there.
The house that peers down at the girl
  and draws her up, and in, bright sun
of revelation; but inside, a smothered world.
  He keeps his shirtsleeves carefully rolled.

I grew up in that house up there,
  where I carry her up and down the stairs,
a sick old woman now, but still not fooled.
  I'm not saying that you shouldn't be
contented here. I'm just doubting that you are.
  Why don't you just get in your car.

 Why don't you just get in your car
  and drive away from here.
Don't climb up to the upper floor,
  don't open up another door.
The hangings swagged and gathered;
  old lady's clothes in the armoire.

My mother and I were more than happy here
  behind the pleated curtain's lace:
her ornate bedroom, me in my place. Snoop
  through the swamp of fringed and floral,
bronze, embroidery, ormolu. Startle
  at the image of yourself, and more.

You'll never understand my love for her.
My mother and I were more than happy here.

Alternative for 1:30:30 > 1:37:16   (page 33)

CATHERINE SMITH
SHE SITS LIKE A BIRD

The battle is over

Norman is no longer

The battle is over

Norman is no longer

The battle is over

Norman is no longer

Norman is no longer

The battle is over

He stole her corpse

The battle is over

He wore her hair

She threw him over

The battle is over

He wore her hair

He was never all Norman

Hid her in the fruit cellar

He dressed in her clothes

The battle is over

He weighted her coffin

The mother has won

You have to go back

Ten years it's been over

She met a new man

You have to go back

She threw him over

Matricide is the most unbearable

His mother took over

He weighted her coffin

He wore her clothes

She wore him down

The mother was jealous

Like a dutiful son

When reality took over

He began to speak for her

She threw him over

He had to speak for her

She sat in the cellar

The mother has won

She asks for a blanket

It's sad when a mother

Has to speak the words

That condemn her own son

She feels a little chill

She sits very quiet

She won't harm her boy

With its innards all padded

The battle is over

She sits very quiet

The battle is over

Norman is over

He wore her hair

The battle is over

He stuffed the birds

She won't harm a fly

She sits like a bird

She won't harm a fly

Norman is over

She won't harm a fly

Alternative for 1:37:17 > The End (page 36)

CAST IN ORDER OF APPEARANCE

Matthew Welton is the author of *The Book of Matthew* and *We needed coffee but…* (Carcanet), and *Waffles* (Eggbox). He teaches at Nottingham University.

Dzifa Benson is a poet, playwright, storyteller, journalist, essayist and, more recently, a fledgling librettist.

Simon Barraclough is the author of the Forward-shortlisted *Los Alamos Mon Amour* (Salt, 2008), *Bonjour Tetris* (Penned in the Margins, 2010) and *Neptune Blue* (Salt, 2011). www.simonbarraclough.com

Heather Phillipson is a poet and artist. Her pamphlet was published by Faber & Faber in 2009. Her debut collection, *Instant-flex 718* (Bloodaxe) will be published in 2013. www.heatherphillipson.co.uk

Richard Price's books include the poetry collections *Lucky Day*, *Rays*, and *Small World* (Carcanet) and the novel *The Island* (Two Ravens). www.hydrohotel.net

Jane Draycott's collections include *Over* (shortlisted for the T.S. Eliot Prize, 2009), *The Night Tree* and *Prince Rupert's Drop* (Oxford Poets/Carcanet). www.janedraycott.org.uk

Emily Berry co-edits the poetry anthology series *Stop Sharpening Your Knives*. Her debut collection is forthcoming from Faber & Faber.

Chris McCabe's poetry books are *The Hutton Inquiry* (2005), *Zeppelins* (2008) and *THE RESTRUCTURE* (2012) all from Salt. He has also written a play for voices *Shad Thames, Broken Wharf* (Penned in the Margins, 2010).

Joe Dunthorne's second novel *Wild Abandon* won the Encore Award and his debut *Submarine* was made into a prize-winning film. His debut poetry pamphlet was published by Faber & Faber. www.joedunthorne.com

Luke Heeley's poems have appeared in the anthologies *Ask for It by Name* and *The Art of Wiring*. His debut collection, *Dust Sheet*, is forthcoming from Salt Publishing.

Isobel Dixon is the author of *The Tempest Prognosticator* (Salt), *A Fold in the Map* (Salt) and *Weather Eye* (Carapace). www.isobeldixon.com

Annie Freud is the author of *A Voids Officer Achieves the Tree Pose* (Donut Press, 2006) and *The Best Man That Ever Was* (Picador, 2007), which won the Dimplex Prize for Poetry. Her second full collection *The Mirabelles* (Picador, 2010) was a Poetry Book Society Choice, and was shortlisted for the T.S. Eliot Prize.

Roddy Lumsden has published seven collections, including *Terrific Melancholy* (Bloodaxe) and *The Bells of Hope* (Penned in the Margins). He is Series Editor for T*he Best British Poetry* and Poetry Editor at Salt Publishing.

Liane Strauss is the author of *Leaving Eden* (Salt), *Frankie, Alfredo,* (Donut) and Head of Poetry in Creative Writing at Birkbeck College, University of London. www.lianestrauss.com

John Stammers' first collection, *Panoramic Lounge-bar*, won the Forward Prize for Best First Collection. His third collection, *Interior Night*, was published by Picador in April 2010.

Catherine Smith's *Lip* (Smith/Doorstop) was shortlisted for the Forward Prize. Her most recent collection, *Otherwhere*, will be published in October 2012. www.catherinesmithwriter.co.uk